Dendrochronology

poems by

Bethanie Humphreys

Finishing Line Press
Georgetown, Kentucky

Dendrochronology

~for Heather, Isabella, Celia, & John
Without your love and support
I would not be

Copyright © 2019 by Bethanie Humphreys
ISBN 978-1-63534-943-6 First Edition
All rights reserved under International and Pan-American Copyright Conventions. No part of this book may be reproduced in any manner whatsoever without written permission from the publisher, except in the case of brief quotations embodied in critical articles and reviews.

ACKNOWLEDGMENTS

Special thanks to the editors of the following publications where these poems, some in earlier versions, first appeared:

American River Review, 2017: "As If Eaten," which was awarded Honorable Mention in the Pacific-Western Division from Community College Humanities Association
American River Review, 2017: "High School Science Experiment"
Found Poetry Review, Volume 10: "Ruminant," now titled "Giraffa"
Here Comes Everyone (UK), 2016: "Mathematical Proof"
NonBinary Review, 2016: "Inverted"
Paperbagwriters.net, 2014: "A Natural History of Desire"
Sacramento Voices Anthology II: "On This Page," now titled "The Art of Sitting Still"
Tule Review, 2013: "On This Page," now titled "The Art of Sitting Still"

Publisher: Leah Maines
Editor: Christen Kincaid
Cover Art: Heather Judy–art, Bethanie Humphreys–photo
Author Photo: Heather Judy
Cover Design: Heather Judy

Printed in the USA on acid-free paper.
Order online: www.finishinglinepress.com
    also available on amazon.com

Author inquiries and mail orders:
Finishing Line Press
P. O. Box 1626
Georgetown, Kentucky 40324
U. S. A.

Table of Contents

Arbor 1
Coloring Eggs 2
The Art of Sitting Still 3
Still Life with Television 4
Hughson 5
Anamnesis 6
If Sylvia Was a Shrike 7
Mathematical Proof 8
High School Science Experiment 10
As If Eaten 12
Cephalopod 14
Eolian-Born 15
Inverted 16
Giraffa 17
My Kind 18
A Natural History of Desire 19
Frog-Skin Leaves 20
While at Your Uncle's Funeral 21
Tree Acoustics 22
Clark's Fork 24
Lepidoptera 25
I Think I Dreamed We Were Birds 26
86 Dead Trees 27
Kintsugi 30
Threading the Needle 31
Notes 32
Additional Acknowledgments 33

ARBOR

These days have passed like ring-lined years in trees.
Swift growth this spring, in stark contrast to dark-
edged rings, marks these writhing winters wrought.
I come to you in temperance. I come to you

between the sheen of it. Early wood,
less dense, the tender inner circle widens.
Hidden in core and limb—an arduous history
rife with drought, sunspots, insect attacks.

Perhaps someone will write of it—the way
to synchronize our dendrochronology—
as if we are more than hypothetical.
But until then, chink a bit from our outer limbs

and read for yourself this drunken season spinning.

COLORING EGGS

When coloring eggs for Easter
when a young ballerina
wants to dance in the kitchen
I hold them soft so
as not to break them

Shell pink, powder purple, whipped-egg yellow
toe and toe and toe

That's how Miss Jeannie does it
she says

She only needs one of my fingers
to twirl and twirl and twirl

With white crayon we draw pictures
revealed by vinegar, color, and time—
silly and sloppy

We don't stop until *everything*
is rainbow, rainbow, rainbow

THE ART OF SITTING STILL

Not many are concerned
with the life cycle of water lilies,

what happens to moldering apples,
hunters' grouse, saffron
sunflower petals curling

into themselves—
these ephemeral models.

The free encyclopedia tells
of Monet's obsession—
a story of light

he limned more than two
hundred times his last thirty years
while slowly going blind.

Not many want to hear
of giant water platters, spatterdocks,
roots anchored in murky soil.

Water lily blooms unfold,
pray for beetles three days,
sink back into mire.

My greatest temptation is
to leave you here and now.

STILL LIFE WITH TELEVISION

I remember watching more
the rectangular space
beneath their bedroom door—
fingers of light
................reaching,

raised voices embroidering air.

As the needle missed its mark,
....threads tangled,
..and my brother and I worried
in beaded silence.

........................We made
them offerings—tiny fists
of wild radish blooms,
pale yellow
with the tracest black-
veined webbing.
....She swallowed,

tried to settle
them, organic and
uneven, bowing under
the weight

of their own heads,
in a throat of cut glass.

HUGHSON

I am from almond orchards, the dust-drenched, irrigated Central Valley, population 3,589

I am from California snow falls every spring when breezes whittle petals from trees' grasp

I am almond trees—curdled crust of bark no good for climbing, only bloody knuckles

I am from cats don't live long around here

I am from gophers burrow beneath levees, soon to be drowned, or meet the shovel's edge

I am from my dad bought a drop calf named Bessie for $50, fed her from a metal bucket with a rubber nipple

I am tule fog thicker than potato soup

I am from waking to a black widow nestled in my curtain sheers

I am from recess soccer games—the white boys let me play, and a Mexican boy offered to hold my hand

I am from no one's gay until they graduate high school

I am from we ate Bessie, but never mentioned our meat by name

ANAMNESIS

I had a volcano once,
the size of my palm.

Subjected
to pressure, heat,
the bone of it silting
into crevice and crease,
rooting into epidermis,
dermis, leaching into
capillary deltas,
bisecting veins, lighting
up nerve endings until
I was on fire.

When it latched onto
metacarpals, carpals,
paralyzed my wrist,
threading radius and ulna,
it was too late.

Whatever dwelled in that
volcano mushroomed with it,
segmentally ribbing
the inner crater,
as it swelled and tongued,
threatening the rim.

IF SYLVIA WAS A SHRIKE

I wonder if I would
fit among them—

wattled jacanas and
giant water bugs

black-tailed prairie dogs
white-footed mice

burying beetles
and bottlenose dolphins

leopards, lions, langurs
baboons

meerkats, pigs, rabbits
and bass.

What was once pathological
as tight-lipped corsets,

now known to be natural
as earthworms eating dirt—

these animals
that eat their young.

MATHEMATICAL PROOF

I never thought to wonder
when it would come.
My breasts tender buttons,
loose t-shirts their natural
language. Dandelion legs,
no slope of hips.

It would come when it came,
and it did. At a gas station pit stop
on our way to Palmdale for turkey,
axioms, cranberry sauce,
and family.

The only herald—a low, dull
backache, I thought just the long
car ride, or my brother
irritating me as I read.

The overflowing trash can and
blackened tile grout wiped clean
when I saw the rust-red spots.

I was thinking the square root of two
is irrational when a finch swooped

through the tiny frosted window,

landed on the ledge near my head.

I looked again.

Is that?

Yes, she said. It is.

Then, am I?

You are, she said.

(The standard of rigor is not absolute.)

HIGH SCHOOL SCIENCE EXPERIMENT

Challenge:
Build a form to protect an egg from a three-story drop

Materials:
Corrugated cardboard
Length of string
Paper napkin
Oyster crackers
One egg

First:
Tuck a handful of crackers
into the napkin's makeshift pocket.
Eat them, one at a time,
remembering your grandmother's
beef stew over egg noodle.

Pick up the egg.
Weigh it in your palm like a cold, unsheathed testicle.
Consider the size of the chicken's vagina.
Wonder if chickens have vaginas.
Feel a bit sorry for it,
then consider your own.

Next:
Tear the cardboard into noodley strips.
Relish the stuttering ease of its demise.
Upon finishing, reconsider whether
dismantling the cardboard
was the best course of action.
Form a soft pile of shreddings.
Perch egg on top.
Watch it shift and lurch
with a hollow knock
onto the surface below.
Check egg for cracks.

Fluff the nest and place egg
more carefully this time.
It doesn't move.
It seems content.
Happy, even.

Then:
You aren't sure what to do with the string.
Tie it around your wrist.
Maybe it will help you remember
something.
Let the long end dangle to the ground
as if your balloon escaped or was set free.
Consider whether you should
be sad the balloon is gone,
or happy it's free.

Meanwhile:
The egg grows warmer.
It begins to sweat a little.

Last:
You figure out what to do.
Put the egg back in the fridge.
Begin to wear enormous, swallowing clothes.
Stop washing your hair, wearing deodorant, make-up.
Speak in grunts and monosyllables.
Sleep as much as possible.
Eat too much, or very little.
Refuse to go outside.
Renounce all artistic endeavors.

And if anyone asks about the egg,
or that three-story drop,
just tell them to mind
their own fucking business.

AS IF EATEN

as if un-knowing scars
could erase the ache sewing
Calla lilies on her tongue

she cannot speak but for petals
drop snow
blanket the present
in constant interruptions

speak as if un-sewing
the present could know
pain but for petals
she cannot drop

Calla lilies like scars
blanket her tongue
in constant snow
interruptions

she can't eat
or erase snow
from constant landscape

interruptions
un-blanket the bruise
drop Calla lilies
spoken scars as if petals
for the present

snow-thickened ache
drops blankets
whitened scars
petals erased
Calla lilies interrupted

she speaks broken
sewing something
into the landscape
as if eaten

eat landscape
unbroken by present
speak of scars
as if wounds can
be erased by snow she
said
by Calla lilies
she said
by a blanket of petals
by something thick and white

CEPHALOPOD

I taste what I touch
but I swim headfirst

no bones to hinder
I pour in and out tight spaces

do not come too close
my defenses are many

this sweet flesh
venomous when threatened

deimatic displays of puffed skin
many dark-ringed eyes

concealment is my safe house
if luck holds you won't see

much more than this ink

EOLIAN-BORN

born with a map
as if
black boots untied
a known
eolian moth
no logical reason
bare
birdless lips
mention
his absence
pooling in puddles of mud
fixate on the tongue
dissolving like a page

dissolving in her palm
there had been order
no words to hide behind
but forgotten language
stuttering flight
luminance unraveled
breastbone heaving
touch down
don't mention
interred questions
slashed with sky
the clouds that arise
in salt water

INVERTED

Inside the rabbit hole, among clotted
soil, shivering roots, an earthworm's holy
paradise, the moon burns black, and not
a soul eats corn. It's perfectly natural
not only mother bears eat their young,
and mitochondria flee their cells. Lowly
mice are king. Minutes highlight gradual
lengthening days, and love's bite is not this pain.

Our skin no barrier, eyes wide, arms flung.
When a girl, not looking, finds soft love
in a girl's raw heart, so it goes with the grain.
Limbs notched in lavender haze, no thistle
to mar their dandelion limbs, hassle
their undomesticated love. Kissed full.

GIRAFFA

six feet tall at birth
I fall five
sever the cord
stand
then walk ten hours

disappear in acacia
I lift the canopy's skirt
with my tongue
purplish-black
thick skin immune
to thorns

I prefer tender greens but
have been known to lick
dried meat from jilted bones

spread my legs to drink
males neck to rule

but I will care for my young
with other mothers

no home but a range
I change friends with the hour

silenced by my own
anatomy

ruminant
I see in color

MY KIND

You do not
make horses bolt
skin puff
turn ring-eyed and scarlet

You let
honey drip
felted leaves
unfold

We go together like
fingers and forks
tongues and bubblegum

We've left behind
apricot seasons
the star thistle of the new

in favor of simple cotton worn soft
pushed and paled at the folds

Not much natural is colorfast

but we find if we forgive them
even weeds wending through
sidewalk cracks can bloom

A NATURAL HISTORY OF DESIRE

In the same family as cinnamon
Camphora, and bay laurel

Up to sixty-six feet tall
Desire grows on a tree

Partially self-pollinating
A long juvenile period

The timing of male and female
Flower phases often differ

Most need climate without frost and high winds
Vulnerable to disease

Native, undomesticated desire
Likely co-evolved with now extinct megafauna

Green-skinned, fleshy
Pear, egg-shaped, or spherical

Desire matures on the tree
But only ripens when plucked

Ready to consume when flesh yields
To gentle pressure

Particularly when pressed
Between fingers and palm

Popular with vegetarians
As a substitute for meat

Sweet but rich, distinct yet subtle
Desire is served raw

FROG-SKIN LEAVES

I want to show you these tiny leaves that look like lily pads, like the skin of the frog that would sit on them, delicate veins lit from behind like stained-glass capillaries arching up the stem.

It's cool here in the shade of the building, cement walls water-stained from morning sprinklers. I want to render for you these leaves, but no pencil and paper, no camera to show you with precision the frog-skinness, how I want to touch them to know if leathery or slick.

Nothing to explain my sitting on the sidewalk thinking of you, frogs, and the lily pads at Giverny we didn't see, just their curved, wall-length translations at l'Orangerie that made me wonder at what point in his descent into blindness did Monet paint these, whether his wife helped him stage the awkward canvas banners outside, whether they ever hurried to dismantle and bring them inside like laundry on the line when sky promised rain.

I promised you a canvas big enough to cover the garage floor. It doesn't rain in the garage.

I want to show you these leaves.

WHILE AT YOUR UNCLE'S FUNERAL

While at your uncle's funeral, when the family is called to assemble for a family photo, your mother grabs your arm and says, "Your sister-in-law thinks you and your girl friend are a couple." Do you:

    a) blink like the proverbial deer in headlights?
    b) be the headlights blazing at the deer?
    c) be the driver that runs her over?
    d) say the no that might be a lie, or just a no to the situation?

While at your uncle's funeral, while waiting for the family to gather for the photo, your mother drags you over to your sister-in-law to "correct her." You:

    a) share the mutual you-know-my-mom, what-the-hell-am-I-supposed-to-say-here look with your sister-in-law.
    b) wait for your mother to repeat what it is she wants you to say.
    c) alternate between raising both eyebrows at your mother, and one eyebrow at your sister-in-law.
    d) continue in awkward silence until she nudges you, and then say, "My mother wants me to tell you we're not together."

While at your uncle's funeral, still waiting for the five non-family members with seven cell phones to take the stupid picture, you:

    a) try not to breathe too hard on the people crowded in around you.
    b) smile, stop smiling, then smile again.
    c) wonder whether you are supposed to smile at your uncle's funeral, even for a family photo.
    d) consider whether it matters, you probably weren't smiling anyway.

TREE ACOUSTICS

Linger over limbs

Every leaf a comma
deserves pause

Topography of age-
thickened bark
crossed over
in long-legged Xs
buckling at their middles

thththththlip limbs thlip
   thlip wind
                thlip

Branches cut
scars like coins oozed
over by crystallized honey

A tree is meant
to be symmetrical
if nothing gets in its way

(Would I be symmetrical
if I didn't get in my own way)
   thththlip I slip

        everymomentacrowd
        for introverted trees

How best to listen
Which sounds most worrisome

Trees take in water through xylem,
bundles of drinking straws
that rely on attractive forces
between water molecules
to lift liquid to the highest leaves

       Is it anthropomorphism
       to say trees cry for help

Increased pressure of sucking
the last drop
from the glass-bottom
can cause xylem to break—
cavitations sound a distinct acoustic pattern
within range of human hearing—

too many can be deadly
to drought-stricken trees

  So many noises unrelated to drought
    so many interruptions

(sometimes I interrupt myself)
   thlip wind thlip

Listen: roots water-knitted

      roots water-dry

      roots awaiting leaves

      leaves, a crown

      leaves: crown of commas

CLARK'S FORK

He told me　　　very little　about salmon fishing on the Feather River
He always told me　everything　according to scripture
He never told me　anything　across the room, the television
　　　　　　　　Something　after dinner, women do the dishes
　　　　　　　　nothing　along the road, the talk, of marriage
　　　　　　　　　　　　amid Petri dishes and sterile medium
　　　　　　　　　　　　among almond orchards
　　　　　　　　　　　　at my brother's basketball games
　　　　　　　　　　　　behind a tree, the belt
　　　　　　　　　　　　below, a lake of fire
　　　　　　　　　　　　beneath the headlight cover, a dead bulb
　　　　　　　　　　　　beside the TV Guide, his bible
　　　　　　　　　　　　between arguments at the dinner table
　　　　　　　　　　　　beyond the foot drop, the double vision
　　　　　　　　　　　　but there was one lucid breakfast
　　　　　　　　　　　　by the road, crops identified
　　　　　　　　　　　　concerning the oil level, a flat tire
　　　　　　　　　　　　down near Clark's Fork, trout fishing
　　　　　　　　　　　　in the last conversation, our only secret,
　　　　　　　　　　　　　　　her name
　　　　　　　　　　　　inside the hospice house
　　　　　　　　　　　　in spite of constricted throats
　　　　　　　　　　　　instead, breathing tubes
　　　　　　　　　　　　into and out of his nose
　　　　　　　　　　　　like a bit of blood leaking out
　　　　　　　　　　　　off radiation, off chemo
　　　　　　　　　　　　on television, the earth
　　　　　　　　　　　　onto a tour of the hospice house
　　　　　　　　　　　　out of that room with the pink drapes
　　　　　　　　　　　　over the rug, I pulled the oxygen tank
　　　　　　　　　　　　past closed doors
　　　　　　　　　　　　through this, a coming together
　　　　　　　　　　　　through it all, her tiny body forming
　　　　　　　　　　　　to contrast the dying, life hurtling on
　　　　　　　　　　　　toward her, this next generation
　　　　　　　　　　　　upon his resignation
　　　　　　　　　　　　with much regret
　　　　　　　　　　　　my child flutters within

LEPIDOPTERA

Luna-girl, you so sweet with no mouthparts
to make you fat and loud.

O' sweet cedar and lavender myths, these oils
do not repel you.

Do you fly among Tiger friends, whose clicks
thwart bats' echolocation?

By moon you fly true, but there
are so many moons.

It's not until you plummet and shift, spiral
and smash against its heat

that you know the true from its foil.

I THINK I DREAMED WE WERE BIRDS

Yardstick ruler strapped
across our shoulders
feathers dyed jewel tones
taped in streamer-fashion
along measurements
that no longer matter

86 DEAD TREES

1. Red bird watching me
2. That I cannot look in the eye
3. The way you say "familiar pain"
4. When a tree dies
5. Measured in time away from him
6. Fingers leave spiral maps of oil and error
7. One can avoid tree wounding
8. By planting in a sheltered location
9. Diminuendo awaiting accent
10. Cross a bridge trying not to think earthquakes
11. Take care when using lawnmowers and tree trimmers
12. Improper pruning
13. I told him I wanted the carrot, not thinking of the cheap
14. Metaphor. He took it down from the ceiling, the real one
15. With fat hooks, he blew off the dust and gave it to me
16. Too much herbicide
17. Held in limbo for observation
18. Both imply holding
19. Both imply dying
20. The skin I peel away after a blister has risen and dried
21. Make sure instructions for application are carefully followed
22. Silver thread unspooling, grapes sugaring, rock salt
23. And Bethanie, as in a longing to dissolve, is longing
24. The usual flour, sugar, butter, of course
25. Soil compaction
26. Recessive skin allele
27. Lack of down means easy bruising
28. Peach rod-armed sorcerers
29. Sent ahead to ward off spectral evils
30. This is a slow tree damage process
31. Pore space reduced, roots don't get enough oxygen
32. Light a match and it's nothing
33. But a plume of black feathers

34. A canyon of bats
35. Panic in a grocery store
36. Red bird watching me
37. Bad planting
38. Ancient pickling methods cannot stop it
39. Unpetaled, her paintbrush down
40. Question-sodden, middle heavy
41. I burst into something like
42. Tiny light through a pinprick
43. Make sure the planting hole is two to three times wider
44. But no deeper than the root ball
45. To hang upside down from, flip and fall down
46. To scrape your knees on the sand beneath from
47. Braille dots read I. Don't. Know.
48. I read too many books
49. Disappear in acacia
50. Lift the canopy's skirt with my tongue
51. Over-watering
52. Under-watering
53. Silenced by my own anatomy
54. In time to protect us, like a syllable
55. Let honey drip, felted leaves unfold
56. Apricot seasons, the star thistle of the new
57. Monitoring soil moisture
58. Drape sinew and flesh over scapular wings
59. Plant hardiness zone
60. Red bird watching me
61. Up to sixty-six feet tall
62. Desire grows on a tree
63. Yields to gentle pressure
64. The persistence of the tick
65. Tock never stopping for a second
66. Glance
67. (Sometimes it hurts to breathe)

68. Painting tree wounds and
69. Filling cavities with concrete
70. As if time was never brick and mortar
71. What happens when a tree dies?
72. Insects invade
73. Animals break apart the tree to eat the insects
74. Fungus and bacteria
75. Back into soil
76. What might
77. Remain standing for another
78. Ten or twenty years
79. Provide valuable habitat
80. Trouble protecting the inner heartwood
81. Heal by compartmentalizing
82. The damage
83. Walls 1-4
84. Begin to fail
85. Marveling at the depth
86. Of our wounds

KINTSUGI

Of course you aren't a backyard pond with koi
caressing cement walls, or lawn that never
fingers far. You're tangled sprawling mint
refusing to leave the warm and ready bed.

Of course you aren't a parlor palm. You welt
and buckle sidewalks, wend through silt and stone.
Break the clay pot. You are thaw and mend
and raw and flesh and scalped wings that fly.

Of course you aren't the loss of light, but Renoir's
black—you'd punch a hole in canvas if someone
told you: "Don't." You are no violet beta
in a tiny blinded bowl. No whim, no knot.

Of course you're not. A cephalopod, no bones
to hinder, venom to the touch. You're scar
and raw and clamshell clasp the tongue, snap
the sternum, let it fly. You are not your body.

Of course you're not.

THREADING THE NEEDLE

All these dangling feelings, this fringe,
this fray—near impossible to thread
through the tiny steel notch.

I anchor my legs, settle into the notch
of your arms as we're pushed to the fringe,
the outer edge—you tuck in my threads.

The strength of even the thinnest thread
is a marvel—like braids of sinew in notch
of scapula, tibia, fibula. And if this fringe

of thread is wetted, fringe stroked, it can be calmed, notched.

NOTES

"Coloring Eggs:" The line, *"Everything is rainbow, rainbow, rainbow,"* is from Elizabeth Bishop's poem, "The Fish."

"Anamnesis" is defined by Merriam-Webster as *1: a recalling to mind: reminiscence; 2: a preliminary case history of a medical or psychiatric patient.*

"Still Life with Television" is inspired by Louise Glück's poem, "Scraps."

"Hughson" is inspired by George Ella Lyon's poem, "Where I'm From."

"If Sylvia Was a Shrike," is inspired by Sylvia Plath's poem, "Winter Landscape, with Rooks."

"Mathematical Proof" is inspired by Rita Dove's poem, "Adolescence II."

"As If Eaten" is inspired by the collected works of Leslie Scalapino.

"Inverted" is inspired by Elizabeth Bishop's poem, "Insomnia," and the rhyme scheme is patterned after, "The Prodigal."

"Tree Acoustics" is inspired by Brenda Hillman's book, *Seasonal Works with Letters on Fire.*

"Lepidoptera" is in response to Elizabeth Bishop's poem, "Man-Moth."

"86 Dead Trees," lines 85 & 86 are inspired by Tony Hoagland's poem, "Jet."

ADDITIONAL ACKNOWLEDGMENTS

I am grateful to so many who shared their time, space, and wisdom to allow me to write these poems:

I especially want to thank Kate Asche for leading, "The Art of the Collection," and fellow classmates Lisa Ludden, Jenny Jiang, Martha Stromberger, Kathy Les, Beth Suter, Marianne Porter, and Heather Judy. Your guidance and comments on editing and arrangement were invaluable. Also to Kate Asche for her other wonderful workshops which inspired poems "Anamnesis" and "Frog-Skin Leaves."

To my *American River Review* family of readers, editors, and friends.

To my stellar American River College creative writing teachers: Michael Spurgeon, Traci Gourdine, Christian Kiefer, Lois Ann Abraham, and David Merson.

To my prosody guru Joshua McKinney, who opened my eyes to the secret code of meter, and whose classes inspired me to write "Arbor," and "Kintsugi," and without whom I would not have met one very special woman.

To the Sacramento Poetry Center and our writing community, the most vibrant and encouraging I've ever known. To Bob Stanley who first welcomed me into the fold and encouraged my interest in the intersection of the visual and literary arts, to Philip Larrea who invited me to do my first featured reading, to Frank Graham for all of his wonderful workshops, one of which inspired me to write "Hughson," and to so many others, on the board and off, who have encouraged and supported me.

To NaPoWriMo for daring me to write a poem a day for the month of April since 2013, and websites such as NaPoWriMo.net for providing the seeds to grow them."

To the Squaw Valley Community of Writers Poetry Workshop attendees and fearless leaders—especially to J. Michael Martinez for giving me the prompt for "High School Science Experiment," and Sharon Olds for pointing out the vagina in that poem is *very important*. Also to Evie Shockley for introducing me to the multiple-choice form I used in "While At My Uncle's Funeral."

To Mark Shea for the priceless gift of flexibility and time.

To the many illustrious poets I will never cease to emulate, and to Heather Judy, the most illustrious poet, artist, and wife, my best friend, best editor, my first reader, and my last.

Bethanie Humphreys is a writer, editor, and mixed media visual artist. She serves as a board member for the Sacramento Poetry Center and curator for the Sacramento Poetry Center Art Gallery.

She is a Squaw Valley Community of Writers Poetry Workshop Alumni, and has a Bachelor of Arts in Spanish from CSU, Sacramento, and a Creative Writing Certificate in Literary Publishing from American River College. She is a California Certified Naturalist through the University of California and will complete leadership training in the Amherst Writers and Artists Method in the summer of 2019. She will begin offering workshops that blur the lines between visual art, creative writing, and science in Fall, 2019.

She enjoys teaching encaustics and recycled papermaking, and her artwork has been in numerous juried and group shows in the Sacramento area, featured in February, 2013 *Sac Bee* as: "top five picks for exhibits to fuel the imagination," and her studio was chosen as curator's pick for Sac Open Studios in 2014.

Editor-in-Chief of the 2015 *American River Review*, and current Associate Editor for *Tule Review*, her poetry, short fiction, and art have appeared in various publications in the U.S. and U.K. including: *Artemis, Nonbinary Review, The Found Poetry Review, American River Review,* and *Sacramento Voice*s.

As a member of Typewriter Nomads, along with Heather Judy, she attends events and types impromptu poems based on questions answered by guests.

www.ingramcontent.com/pod-product-compliance
Lightning Source LLC
LaVergne TN
LVHW041600070426
835507LV00011B/1211